Helen KELLER

Break Down the Walls!

by Margaret Fetty

CONSULTANT
Helen Selsdon
Archivist
Helen Keller Archives at the American Foundation for the Blind

BEARPORT
PUBLISHING

New York, New York

Credits

Cover and title page, New York Times Co./Getty Images; 4, Used by permission
Perkins School for the Blind, Watertown, MA; 5, Library of Congress; 6, American
Foundation for the Blind; 7, Larry Gillentine; 8–9 (all 3 photos), American Foundation
for the Blind; 10, Larry Gillentine; 11T, Used by permission Perkins School for the
Blind, Watertown, MA; 11B, American Foundation for the Blind; 12–14 (all 3 photos),
Used by permission Perkins School for the Blind, Watertown, MA; 15, American
Foundation for the Blind; 16, ©Craig Hammell/CORBIS; 17T, Used by permission
Perkins School for the Blind, Watertown, MA; 17B, American Foundation for the Blind;
18, Used by permission Perkins School for the Blind, Watertown, MA; 19, Library of
Congress; 20–21 (both), American Foundation for the Blind; 22, Used by permission
Perkins School for the Blind, Watertown, MA; 23–26T (all 4 photos), American
Foundation for the Blind; 26B, LBJ Library Photo by Unknown; 27, Bettmann/CORBIS.

Publisher: Kenn Goin
Project Editor: Adam Siegel
Creative Director: Spencer Brinker
Original Design: Fabia Wargin

Library of Congress Cataloging-in-Publication Data
Fetty, Margaret.
  Helen Keller : break down the walls! / by Margaret Fetty.
     p. cm. — (Defining moments. Overcoming challenges)
  Includes bibliographical references and index.
  ISBN-13: 978-1-59716-271-5 (library binding)
  ISBN-10: 1-59716-271-X (library binding)
  ISBN-13: 978-1-59716-299-9 (pbk.)
  ISBN-10: 1-59716-299-X (pbk.)
  1. Keller, Helen, 1880–1968. 2. Blind-deaf women—United States—Biography—
Juvenile literature. I. Title. II. Series.

  HV1624.K4F48 2007
  362.4'1092—dc22

                              2006005855

For more information, write to Bearport Publishing Company, Inc.,
101 Fifth Avenue, Suite 6R, New York, New York 10003.
Printed in the United States of America.

10 9 8 7 6 5 4 3 2 1

Table of Contents

An Amazing Speech

Helen stood before a crowded room in Montclair, New Jersey. She was 32 years old. For the first time in her life, she was giving a **lecture** to a large group of people. Helen was terrified. Her voice was rough. She spoke in a whisper. At times, it was hard to understand her. The audience had to listen carefully.

A poster for Helen's first speaking tour in 1913

Helen's speech amazed the audience. It was the first **public** talk given by Helen Keller, a woman who had been **deaf** and **blind** for most of her life.

Helen Keller around 1914, a year after she gave her first speech

Helen could tell when the audience liked her speech. Their clapping hands would cause the floor to **vibrate**. She could feel the vibrations with her feet.

A Mysterious Illness

It took great **courage** for Helen to speak in front of a crowd. Yet Helen had an important message to share. She wanted people to know that blind and deaf people should get an education. Not being able to see or hear was something Helen knew a lot about. After all, she had been blind and deaf since she was 19 months old.

Helen could see and hear when she was a baby.

Baby Helen

Helen grew up in this house in Tuscumbia, Alabama.

When Helen was born on June 27, 1880, she was a healthy baby. Then, in February 1882, a mysterious illness made Helen very sick. She had a high fever. When the sickness ended, Helen was not able to see or hear.

A Dark and Silent World

Since Helen could not hear or see people speak, she did not learn how to talk. Helen used her hands and body to **communicate**. If Helen wanted bread, she would pretend to cut slices and spread butter. If she wanted someone to come with her, she would pull on the person.

Captain Arthur Keller,
Helen's father

Kate Keller,
Helen's mother

Helen helped do chores around the house. She folded the family's clean clothes and put them away.

Helen around the age of seven

Even in her dark and silent world, Helen knew she was different. By feeling faces, she could tell that people moved their lips to communicate. Helen became **frustrated** because she could not do the same. As a result, Helen grew wild. She often kicked and screamed in anger.

Wild Child

Helen's behavior got worse as she got older. When she was five years old, Helen hit people when she was upset. She broke lamps and dishes. During meals, Helen ate food from other people's plates. Everyone let Helen do what she wanted, to keep her from throwing **tantrums**.

Helen often walked around the dining room using her fingers to take the food she wanted from other people's plates.

Kate Keller, Helen's mother, knew that her daughter was smart. Mrs. Keller had read a book about a blind and deaf girl named Laura Bridgman. Laura had been taught to communicate by using her fingers to spell words. Mrs. Keller believed that Helen could learn to use this **manual alphabet** just like Laura.

Laura Bridgman, the first blind and deaf person to be taught to use the manual alphabet

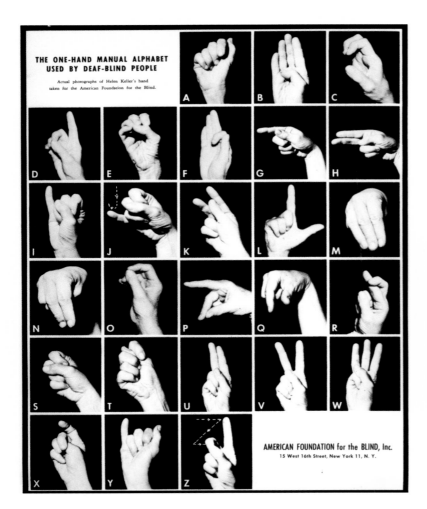

In the manual alphabet, fingers are shaped to stand for each letter of the alphabet. When the finger shapes for different letters are put together, they form words.

Help for Helen

Hoping to help Helen, the Kellers visited many doctors. Finally, they went to see Dr. Alexander Graham Bell, a well-known teacher of deaf students. He suggested that the Kellers write to the Perkins Institution for the Blind in Boston. The school could find a teacher for Helen.

Alexander Graham Bell invented the telephone. His idea for this invention began as a hearing aid for deaf people.

Helen and Dr. Bell became good friends. This photo was taken of them in 1902.

Anne Sullivan was 20 years old when she became Helen's teacher.

On March 3, 1887, the Kellers prepared the house for Helen's new teacher. Helen sensed the excitement. She wondered what was happening. The six-year-old girl waited on the porch.

When Helen felt footsteps, she held out her hand. She expected to touch her mother. Instead, she felt Anne Sullivan's arms around her. A surprised Helen tried to break free.

A Breakthrough!

Anne began teaching Helen right away. She gave the young girl a doll. Then Anne used her fingers to shape the letters *d-o-l-l* in Helen's hand. Helen repeated the finger shapes. Yet Helen's face looked puzzled. She did not understand that her fingers spelled a word.

Helen with her dog Jumbo in 1887, the year that Anne came to teach her

Anne did not give up. She kept finger-spelling words into Helen's hand. Finally, on April 5, 1887, Anne took Helen to a pump. She held Helen's hand in the splashing water. Anne quickly spelled *w-a-t-e-r*. Helen stood still. The look on her face changed. At last, she understood that the finger movements named things!

This is the pump where Helen learned the word "water."

Anne Sullivan had trouble seeing when she was young. She had many operations during her lifetime. A few improved her sight. Yet she still could not see well throughout her life.

An Eager Learner

Now that Helen could communicate, she was very eager to learn about her world. Within six months, Helen knew how to finger-spell more than 600 words.

Helen learned how to communicate in other ways, too. During the summer, Helen was taught to read and write Braille. In Braille, different patterns of raised dots stand for the letters of the alphabet. People use their fingers to "read" the words.

Many books are published in Braille.

Louis Braille, a blind French student, invented the Braille alphabet system by the time he was 15 years old.

Helen also learned how to write with a pencil. She wrote letters to people all over the country. Some of her letters were published in newspapers and magazines. Helen became famous after people read about her amazing life.

Helen around the age of eight reading a Braille book

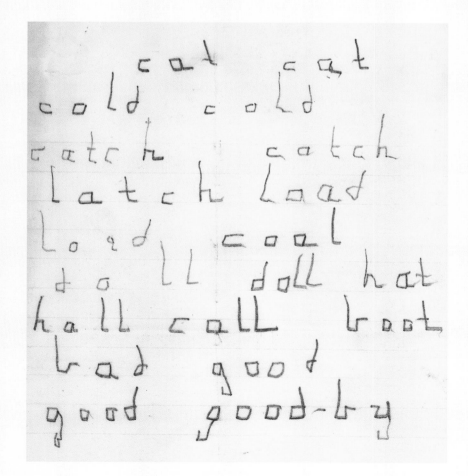

Early writing by Helen, a week before she turned seven

The Impossible

When Helen was nine years old, she found out that a deaf and blind girl had learned how to talk. Helen wanted to learn how to speak, too. So she began speech lessons. At the end of her first lesson, she could say the sounds for *a, i, m, p, s,* and *t.*

To learn how to speak, Helen would put her hand inside her teacher's mouth to feel the position of the lips and tongue when different sounds were made.

Helen and Anne sometimes sat in the branches of trees during their lessons. Even when Helen was older, the two could be found reading in a tree.

Helen "lip-reading" with Anne in 1897

Helen was also taught to "lip-read" so that she could understand spoken words. By feeling the speaker's lips and the vibrations in the nose and throat, she knew what a person was saying.

Then, in 1900, Helen did the impossible. She began taking classes at Radcliffe College. No blind and deaf person had ever been a student there before.

Earning a Living

College was a challenge for Helen. Few of the books were written in Braille. So Anne had to spell all the words into Helen's hand. Yet with Anne's help, Helen graduated with honors in 1904.

Now Helen was **determined** to earn a living. In college, she had written magazine articles about herself. So Helen decided to write more about her life and thoughts.

Helen was the first blind and deaf person to graduate from college.

In 1903, the articles Helen had written about her life were published as a book, *The Story of My Life*. The book has been translated into more than 50 languages.

Helen learned to play chess. Here she is playing against Anne (right).

Helen quickly became interested in helping others. Since she was famous, people listened to her. Helen helped organize schools to teach job skills to the blind. She also supported efforts to get women the right to vote.

The Stage Life

Helen did not make enough money writing. So in 1913, she began to give lectures with Anne about her life. People paid to hear Helen talk. She spoke about helping the blind and deaf. Her lectures helped people understand the problems of the **disabled**.

In 1919, Helen starred in Deliverance, a silent movie that told the story of her life.

In 1920, someone asked Helen to do a vaudeville act. Vaudeville was a show where singers, dancers, and **comedians** performed. Helen liked being on stage, so she happily agreed. During the show, Helen and Anne talked about Helen's life. They let people ask questions. Helen gave funny answers. People enjoyed the act.

Helen and Anne did a vaudeville act from 1920 to 1924.

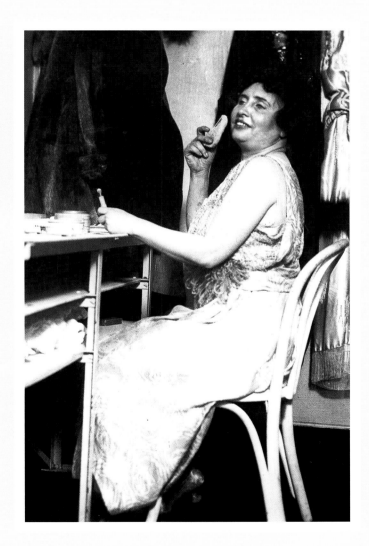

Helen learned to put on her own makeup before going on the vaudeville stage.

Speaking Out for the Blind

In 1924, Helen was asked to help raise money for one of her favorite causes—the blind. The American Foundation for the Blind wanted to educate people on **preventing** blindness. They also wanted to care for and teach those who were blind.

Helen met many presidents in her lifetime. Here she is around 1926 with President Calvin Coolidge.

Helen (left), Anne (center), Polly (right), and Helen's Great Dane around 1932

For the next several years, Helen and Anne traveled around the country giving speeches. Helen was determined "to help others break down the walls of darkness."

After a while, Anne's health began to fail. She became unable to tour. On October 20, 1936, Anne Sullivan died.

A World Champion

After Anne's death, Helen was very sad and lonely. Yet she still traveled to other countries with Polly. She still spoke about educating the blind. In 1961, a **stroke** made her weak. She could not lecture anymore. Seven years later, on June 1, 1968, Helen Keller died.

Helen traveled to Africa in 1951 and received a shield as a gift.

In 1964, Helen received the Presidential Medal of Freedom, the highest honor given to an American citizen.

Helen worked for almost 50 years to help disabled people.

People around the world will always remember Helen as a brave woman. She spent most of her life helping others. Her work truly knocked down many walls—walls that kept her world silent and dark, and walls that kept the disabled from enjoying a successful life.

Just the Facts

- Helen always called Anne Sullivan "Teacher."

- Hot dogs were one of Helen's favorite foods.

- Helen enjoyed music. She used her fingers to touch an instrument, or the throat and cheek of a singer. She felt the vibrations, which helped her learn if the music was high or low.

Timeline

Here are some important events in Helen Keller's life.

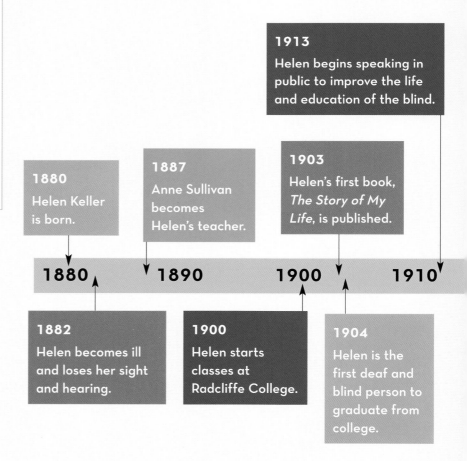

1880
Helen Keller is born.

1887
Anne Sullivan becomes Helen's teacher.

1903
Helen's first book, *The Story of My Life*, is published.

1913
Helen begins speaking in public to improve the life and education of the blind.

1880   **1890**   **1900**   **1910**

1882
Helen becomes ill and loses her sight and hearing.

1900
Helen starts classes at Radcliffe College.

1904
Helen is the first deaf and blind person to graduate from college.

■ Helen loved animals. She often had pet dogs. She also enjoyed riding horses.

■ In 1955, Helen won an Oscar award for a movie that was made about her life, *Helen Keller in Her Story*.

■ In her lifetime, Helen visited 39 countries.

■ Helen wrote ten books and many articles and speeches during her life.

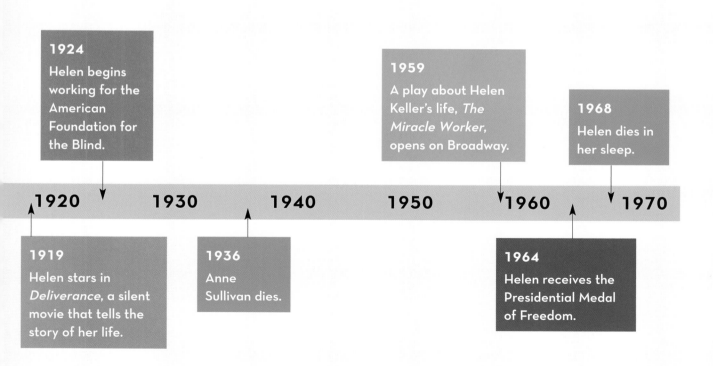

1924
Helen begins working for the American Foundation for the Blind.

1959
A play about Helen Keller's life, *The Miracle Worker*, opens on Broadway.

1968
Helen dies in her sleep.

1920   **1930**   **1940**   **1950**   **1960**   **1970**

1919
Helen stars in *Deliverance*, a silent movie that tells the story of her life.

1936
Anne Sullivan dies.

1964
Helen receives the Presidential Medal of Freedom.

Glossary

blind (BLINDE) not able to see

comedians (kuh-MEE-dee-uhnz) people who make others laugh by telling jokes or acting in a funny way

communicate (kuh-MYOO-nuh-kate) to share information, ideas, feelings, and thoughts

courage (KUR-ij) bravery

deaf (DEF) not able to hear

determined (di-TUR-mind) had a strong will to do something

disabled (diss-AY-buhld) people who are not able to do things, often because an injury or a sickness has hurt their bodies

frustrated (FRUHSS-trate-id) helpless and angry

lecture (LEK-chur) a speech

manual alphabet (MAN-yoo-uhl AL-fuh-bet) a form of communication for the deaf in which fingers are used to shape the letters of the alphabet

preventing (pri-VENT-ing) stopping from happening

public (PUHB-lik) an event taking place that is open to the community

stroke (STROHK) the breaking or blocking of a blood vessel in the brain that causes the loss of feeling, movement, or thought

tantrums (TAN-truhmz) angry crying, kicking, and screaming

vibrate (VYE-brate) to move up and down or back and forth quickly

Bibliography

Herrmann, Dorothy. *Helen Keller: A Life.* Chicago: University of Chicago Press (1999).

Keller, Helen. *The Story of My Life.* New York: Bantam Classics (1990).

Lawlor, Laurie. *Helen Keller: Rebellious Spirit.* New York: Holiday House (2001).

Read More

Markham, Lois. *Helen Keller.* New York: Franklin Watts (1993).

Sabin, Francene. *The Courage of Helen Keller.* Mahwah, NJ: Troll Communications (1982).

Sullivan, George. *Helen Keller (In Their Own Words).* New York: Scholastic (2001).

Learn More Online

Visit these Web sites to learn more about Helen Keller:

www.afb.org/braillebug/helen_keller_bio.asp
www.afb.org/braillebug/hkmuseum.asp
www.kidskonnect.com/HelenKeller/HelenKellerHome.html
www.perkins.org/area.php?id=3

Index

About the Author

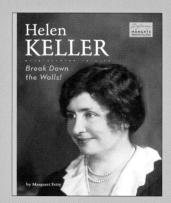

MARGARET FETTY has been a writer and editor of educational materials for more than 15 years. She has written many books for young readers.